I0004175

Reactive Programming

Basics

Starting Reactive in an Easy Way

By John Rhynes

Table of Contents

Disclaimer

While all attempts have been made to verify the information provided in this book, the author does assume any responsibility for errors, omissions, or contrary interpretations of the subject matter contained within. The information provided in this book is for educational and entertainment purposes only. The reader is responsible for his or her own actions and the author does not accept any responsibilities for any liabilities or damages, real or perceived, resulting from the use of this information.

The trademarks that are used are without any consent, and the publication of the trademark is without permission or backing by the trademark owner. All trademarks and brands within this book are for clarifying purposes only and are the owned by the owners themselves, not affiliated with this document. **

Introduction

Changes are always made to applications. In most cases, these changes are not expected at all. Data flows also need to be propagated throughout software applications so as to keep each part updated and in a consistent state. As a programmer, you should come up with a user app with an interactive user interface. This can be achieved with Reactive programming.

Chapter 1- A Brief Overview of Reactive Programming

This refers to a programming paradigm which revolves around propagation of change and data flows. It makes it easy for us to express both dynamic and static data flows in the programming language which we are using, and the underlying model of execution will propagate the changes through our data flow automatically.

Reactive programming was developed to provide programmers with a mechanism to create their user interfaces for apps in an easy manner, and make these as interactive as possible. Although it is a general programming paradigm, it also supports animations in systems which are real type.

For those who use the model-view-controller architecture in programming, this paradigm can make it possible for the changes made to the underlying model to be reflected in the view, and the reverse is also true. The Reactive programming languages are many, and these range from the explicit languages to the implicit languages, whereby in the explicit ones, we use arrows to set up data flows while in the implicit ones, we use language constructs.

Chapter 2- Callback Hell

Consider the example given below

```
def keywordOccurrences(urls: List[String], keyword:
String):

  List[(String, Int)] = {

  urls map { url =>

    val html = fetchUrl(url)

    val dom = parseHtmlToDOM(html)

    val count = keywordOccurrencesInDOM(dom,
keyword)

    (url, count)

  }

}
```

In the above case, we have a single-threaded synchronous code. The function *"keywordOccurrences"* will take in a URL and a list of keywords, and then fetch the HTML which is behind the URL. The HTML will then be passed into a representation of DOM, and then proceed to count the number of occurrences of the keyword in each of the pages.

It is easy for you to understand the code, as the operations are performed one after another, and the specified order has to be followed. However, the procedure is not very effective, as each call to the *"fecthUrl"* will be independent from each another, and this makes it easy for us to parallelize these operations, but the code in our case will execute these in a serial manner.

Also, each operation on the method *"fecthUrl"* will involve network IO and will cause a blockage on the execution thread as we wait for the IO to complete.

With an asynchronous callback-based approach, the code can be implemented as follows:

```scala
def keywordOccurrencesAsync(

  urls: List[String],

  keyword: String,

  successHandler: (List[(String, Int)]) => Unit,

  errorHandler: (Throwable) => Unit): Unit = {


  // access to the shared variables will need

  // to be synchronized, and this will add an even more
  complexity

  var resAccumulator = List[(String, Int)]()

  var isUrlCompleted = urls

  .foldLeft(HashMap[String, Boolean]()) {

   (acc, url) =>

    acc.updated(url, false)

  }


  urls map { url =>

   fetchUrlAsync(

   url,

   successHandler = { html =>
```

```
parseHtmlToDOMAsync(

  html,

  successHandler = { dom =>

    countWordOccurrencesInDOMAsync(

      dom,

      keyword,

      successHandler = { count =>

        // adding the result to our accumulator

        resAccumulator    =    (url,    count)    ::
resAccumulator

        // updating the state to denote that the url is
completed

        isUrlCompleted                              =
isUrlCompleted.updated(url, true)


        // checking if all the urls have been completed

        // if it's the case, invoke our top success
handler

        val allDone = isUrlCompleted

              .map { case(key, value) => value }

              .reduce { (a, b) => a && b }

        if (allDone) {
```

```
            successHandler(resAccumulator)

        }

        },

        errorHandler)

    },

    errorHandler)

},

errorHandler)

}

}
```

In this case, each of the *"Async"* function will do an immediate return, and the process of execution will return as the network IO or any other type of computation will be underway. Callback functions have to be passed as arguments so as to handle cases when the operation becomes successful and in any case an error occurs.

The callbacks themselves have to be executed after the processing of the operation has been completed.

With such an approach, the system resources will be used efficiently, but the following are some of the limitations associated with the approach:

- Shared state variables should be used, and access to these variables should be synchronized. In our case, these variables include "resAccumulator" and "isUrlCompleted."

- Each step in the asynchronous processing needs a nested callback and this will finally lead to a "callback hell."

- It is hard for anyone to read and understand the code.

Chapter 3- Futures and promises

The good thing about having a synchronous code such as in our previous case is that a function such as *"fetchUrl"* will return a string which will in turn be used by other functions in their computations. This always causes the code to be easy to read and understand.

To achieve the same with an asynchronous code, we use *"futures."* A future is an object which is used for the purpose of expressing the result of an asynchronous computation, and this might be a variable which is not currently available, but it will be available in the future. With this, the asynchronous version of the *"fetchUrl"* will return *"Future[string]"* type, and this will then be used in the synchronous-looking code, and we will not have to worry about whether the string type will be available.

Promise objects are just utility objects which make it easy for us to construct futures. Consider the code given below:

```
def fetchUrl(url: String): Future[String] = {
  val p = Promise[String]()
  fetchUrlAsync(url,
    successHandler = { html => p.success(html) },
    errorHandler = { error => p.failure(error) })
  p.future
}
```

In the example given above, the *"fetchUrl"* will call the counterpart *"fetchUrlAsync,"* which is based on callback, and a success handler is present which will complete the promise *"p"* with a success and failure handler which will return the *"p"* with a failure. The function will then extract a *"future"* out of the Promise *"p,"* and then return it to our caller. In Reactive programming, it is a common practice for us to wrap code which is callback-based by use of promise objects so as to get a future object. That is what has happened in our code here.

The functions "keywordOccurrencesInDOM" and "parseHtmlToDOM" will be refactored similarly so as to the "Future[DOM]" and "Future[Int]."

Map/filter/reduce hell

The *"future"* trait is used for defining higher-order functions such as the *"flatMap,, "map," "fold," "reduce,"* and *"filter."* When we compare these functions to the ones contained in *"list,"* they are not exactly the same, but they can be said to be similar. An example of this is when *"flatMap"* has been defined on *"Future [T]."* This should be applied to a function which will take *"T"* as the argument and then return *"Future[S]"* flattening the result which is "Future[Future[S]]" to get a single *"Future[S]."*

With higher-order functions, it becomes easy for us to return functions which will return futures by use of familiar functional programming patterns. Consider the code given below, which best demonstrates this:

```scala
import scala.concurrent.{ Future, Promise }

import scala.concurrent.ExecutionContext.Implicits.global
def keywordOccurrences(urls: List[String], keyword: String):
  Future[List[(String, Int)]] = {

  // partially applying keywordOccurrencesInDOM
  val keywordOccurrencesInDOM = keywordOccurrencesInDOM(_: DOM, keyword)

  // expression will evaluate to List[Future[(String, Int)]
  val listOfFutures = urls
    .map { url =>
      fetchUrl(url)
```

```
.flatMap(parseHtmlToDOM)

.flatMap(keywordOccurrencesInDOM)

.map { count => (url, count) } }


// transforming the List[Future[(String, Int)] to get
Future[List[(String, Int)]]

Future.sequence(listOfFutures)

}
```

The *"keywordOccurences"* in the above case will perform a *"flatMap"* on the outcome from *"fetchUrl"* over *"keywordOccurrencesInDOM"* and *"parseHtmlToDOM"* and the result is mapped to a URL pair and count and this will give us "Future[(String, Int)]."

We have called the "Future.sequence" so as to transform the list of the "Future[(String, Int)]" into a future of the "List[(String, Int)]."

The above code appears to be a bit clearer than the example on callback. However, you have to learn that each of the functions in the above example has been created in a way to take the output of the preceding function. We may not have access to the real-world APIs, but we may need to process the output from a function before making it proceed to the next function. This means that in the real-world code, the code could become complicated as a result of the addition of more steps for further processing.

When Reactive code has been composed with higher-order functions, it does not become purely functional. However, it involves side effects through file system or network IO.

Macros

The library "Scala Async" usually provides us with "await" and "async" macros. These macros help us to write asynchronous code in a more efficient manner and more directly, and this is done in the same way that the asynchronous code was coded in our previous example.

The approach to this is that the asynchronous code has to be wrapped within an async block and each computation which will result into a future with the await block. The computation on the block for wait will have to be suspended until completion of the corresponding future is done, but there will not be performance penalties, and it will have to be done in a non-blocking manner.

Consider the code given below, which best illustrates this:

```scala
import scala.concurrent.{ Future, Promise }

import

scala.concurrent.ExecutionContext.Implicits.global

import scala.async.Async.{ async, await }


def keywordOccurrences(urls: List[String], keyword:
String):
 Future[List[(String, Int)]] = {


 // listOfFutures will evaluate to type
List[Future[(String, Int)]
 val listOfFutures = urls

  .map { url => async {

   // html, dom and numberOfOccurrences values
are of type String,

   // DOM, and the Int respectively

   val html = await { fetchUrl(url) }

   val dom = await { parseHtmlToDOM(html) }
```

```
    val count = await {
keywordOccurrencesInDOM(dom, keyword) }

    (url, count)

  }

}


// transforming List[Future[(String, Int)] to the
Future[List[(String, Int)]]

  Future.sequence(listOfFutures)

}
```

The code given above is almost similar to the asynchronous one given previously, but it has reflected our intent more directly, and it looks to be natural.

Chapter 4- Implicit and Explicit Declarations

Reactive programming involves a set of reactions to a set of events which usually happen over a specified period of time. But you should learn how to set up the relationships.

In some programming languages and frameworks, one is provided with some tools which can help us set such relationships explicitly. In some other languages, the connections will have to be setup implicitly so that we can react to the changes that we need.

Explicit

For web developers, you must be experienced in Reactive programming since you are used to implementing event handlers. In JavaScript, one can set up listeners which will help them react to the user inputs.

Consider a situation in which we have a button and we need to alert the user once the button has been clicked. The connection can be done by use of a simple JavaScript as shown in the code given below:

```javascript
var alertUser = function() {
  alert('You have clicked the button');
}
document.getElementById('magic-button').onclick=
function() {
  alertUser();
}
```

What we have done is that we have used the *"onClick"* function on our DOM element, and a function has been set up which will be called once the button has been clicked. The action is that once the button has been clicked, the user will be alerted. With that, the connection will have been set explicitly between clicking on the button and alerting of the user.

Implicit

Because Reactive programming has been found to be very helpful, many frameworks have implemented the process of creating automatic bindings so that they can automatically react to changes to the system.

Consider the React component given below which has a state variable named *"name,"*The component will render another component referred to as *"userWidget,"* and then pass the name to it. The React will then automatically bind the variable named *"name"* in the component to the name which has been passed down to the *"userWidget."* This means that we change the value of the variable in this case, Reeact will have to react to it by triggering the rendering of the element *"userWidget."* Consider the code given below, which shows how this can be done:

```
React.createCreate({
  getDefaultState: function() {
    return {
```

```
      name: 'George'
    }
  },

  render: function() {
   return (
    <div>
     <h1>User Information</h1>
     <UserWidget name=this.state.name />
    </div>
   );
  }
});
```

Chapter 5- Stream Processing

In Reactive programming, streams provide us with a mechanism on how to process asynchronous streams with a non-blocking back pressure. For this to be accomplished, efforts are needed during runtime and network protocols.

In an asynchronous system, we need to have a special system which will help us handle streams of data whose volume cannot be predetermined. It is necessary for us to control how resources are consumed so that a data source which is fast does not overwhelm the destination of our stream. Asynchrony is very important for the purpose of enabling resources to be used in a parallel manner on multiple CPU cores or collaborating network hosts in a single machine.

Reactive streams are very important for governing how stream data is exchanged across an asynchronous boundary. This can be thought of as passing threads or a thread-pool, and our aim is to ensure that the receiving end is not forced so as to buffer an arbitrary data of a certain amount. This means that back pressure is part of this model for ensuring that the queues mediate between the threads which are bounded. In case the communication of the back pressure is synchronous, the benefits of the asynchronous processing will be negated. This means that we have to be careful so as to mandate fully asynchronous and non-blocking for the behavior of implementation of the implementation of Reactive streams.

The intention of this specification is to come up with many similar implementations, and if you adhere to the necessary rules, interoperation will be smooth, and the benefits of stream processing will be preserved.

Scope

In Reactive streams, the scope is to look for the minimal set of the interfaces, protocols, and methods which will be used for describing the necessary entities and operations so as to achieve streams which are goal-asynchronous with a non-blocking back pressure.

End-user protocol binding APIs or DSLs are not part of the scope, and these have been left out deliberately so that different implementations of these can be supported, and these normally make use of different programming languages.

Chapter 6- Using Vert.x for Reactive Programming

Vert.x was developed for the purpose of implementing an event bus, and this facilitates communication between the different parts of an app which can communicate in a thread/non-blocking manner. This was developed so as to make use of the multi-core processors of today and the concurrent demands which are very high.

We want to demonstrate this by creating a REST API using Spring Boot, Spring Data JPA, and Spring REST. The Spring configuration class is shown below:

@SpringBootApplication

@EnableJpaRepositories

@EnableTransactionManagement

@Slf4j

public class MyApp {

   public static void main(String[] args) {

```java
    ApplicationContext ctx =
SpringApplication.run(MyApp.class, args);

    System.out.println("Need to inspect the beans
which are provided by Spring Boot:");

    String[] beans = ctx.getBeanDefinitionNames();

    Arrays.sort(beans);

    for (String beanName : beans) {

        System.out.println(beanName);

    }

}


    @Bean

    public DataSource dataSource() {

    EmbeddedDatabaseBuilder builder = new
EmbeddedDatabaseBuilder();

    return

builder.setType(EmbeddedDatabaseType.HSQL).buil

d();

    }
```

```java
@Bean

public EntityManagerFactory

entityManagerFactory() {

    HibernateJpaVendorAdapter vAdapter = new
HibernateJpaVendorAdapter();

    vAdapter.setGenerateDdl(true);


    LocalContainerEntityManagerFactoryBean
factory = new
LocalContainerEntityManagerFactoryBean();

    factory.setJpaVendorAdapter(vAdapter);


factory.setPackagesToScan("com.zanclus.data.entitie

s");

    factory.setDataSource(dataSource());

    factory.afterPropertiesSet();


    return factory.getObject();
}


@Bean
```

```java
public PlatformTransactionManager
transManager(final EntityManagerFactory emf) {

    final JpaTransactionManager txManager = new
JpaTransactionManager();

    txManager.setEntityManagerFactory(emf);

    return txManager;

  }

}
```

In the above case, we have some Spring Boot annotations at the top. These annotations will provide us with injectable objects which will be used in our other classes.

The Router class will allow us to make use of a fluent API for definition of HTTP URLs, header filters, and methods for the purpose of request handling. Consider the example given below:

```java
@PostConstruct
  public void start() throws Exception {

    Router router = Router.router(vertx);

    router.route().handler(BodyHandler.create());
```

```java
router.get("/c1/customer/:id")

    .produces("application/json")

    .blockingHandler(this::getCustomerById);

router.put("/v1/customer")

    .consumes("application/json")

    .produces("application/json")

    .blockingHandler(this::addCustomer);

router.get("/c1/customer")

    .produces("application/json")

    .blockingHandler(this::getAllCustomers);

vertx.createHttpServer().requestHandler(router::accept).listen(8080);
}
```

We have defined the HTTP method, the header "Accept," and the header for "Content-Type." The handling of the request has been handled via the method *blockingHandler.* The next code for this is given below:

```java
private void newCustomer(RoutingContext rc) {

    try {

        String body = rc.getBodyAsString();

        Customer customer = mapper.readValue(body,
Customer.class);

        Customer saved = dao.save(customer);

        if (saved!=null) {

rc.response().setStatusMessage("Accepted").setStatu
sCode(202).end(mapper.writeValueAsString(saved))
;

        } else {

            rc.response().setStatusMessage("Bad

Request").setStatusCode(400).end("Bad Request");

        }

    } catch (IOException e) {

        rc.response().setStatusMessage("Server
Error").setStatusCode(500).end("Server Error");

        log.error("Server error", e);

    }

}
```

```java
    private void obtainCustomerById(RoutingContext
rc) {
    log.info("Requesting for a single customer");
    Long id =
Long.parseLong(rc.request().getParam("id"));
    try {
        Customer customer = dao.findOne(id);
        if (customer==null) {
            rc.response().setStatusMessage("Not
Found").setStatusCode(404).end("Not Found");
        } else {

rc.response().setStatusMessage("OK").setStatusCode
(200).end(mapper.writeValueAsString(dao.findOne(
id)));

        }
    } catch (JsonProcessingException jpe) {
        rc.response().setStatusMessage("Server
Error").setStatusCode(500).end("Server Error");
        log.error("Server error", jpe);
    }
```

```java
}

    private void obtainAllCustomers(RoutingContext
rc) {

    log.info("Requesting for all the customers");

    List customers =
StreamSupport.stream(dao.findAll().spliterator(),
false).collect(Collectors.toList());

    try {

rc.response().setStatusMessage("OK").setStatusCode
(200).end(mapper.writeValueAsString(customers));

    } catch (JsonProcessingException jpe) {

        rc.response().setStatusMessage("Server
Error").setStatusCode(500).end("Server Error");

        log.error("Server error", jpe);

    }

    }
```

The above code is too much, and it cannot be compared to any

Spring annotation and class you might think of.

The Vert.x web library has been used for the purpose of improving the scalability and concurrency of our app. However, the Vert.x event bus can be used for the purpose of improving things a bit more. Request processing can be handled with much efficiency if we separate the database operations.

The class "*CustomerEndPoints*" should be as follows:

@PostConstruct

   public void start() throws Exception {

     log.info("CustomerVerticle has been created successfully");

     DeploymentOptions deployOptions = new DeploymentOptions().setWorker(true).setMultiThre aded(true).setInstances(4);

vertx.deployVerticle("java-spring:com.zanclus.verticles.CustomerWorker",

 deployOptions, res -> {

```java
        if (res.succeeded()) {

            Router router = Router.router(vertx);

router.route().handler(BodyHandler.create());
            final DeliveryOptions options = new
DeliveryOptions()
                .setSendTimeout(2000);
            router.get("/c1/customer/:id")
                .produces("application/json")
                .handler(rc -> {
                    options.addHeader("method",
"obtainCustomer")
                        .addHeader("id",
rc.request().getParam("id"));

vertx.eventBus().send("com.zanclus.customer", null,
options, reply ->
handleReply(reply, rc));
                });
            router.put("/c1/customer")
```

```java
            .consumes("application/json")

            .produces("application/json")

            .handler(rc -> {

                options.addHeader("method",
"newCustomer");


vertx.eventBus().send("com.zanclus.customer",
rc.getBodyAsJson(), options,

reply -> handleReply(reply, rc));

            });

        router.get("/c1/customer")

            .produces("application/json")

            .handler(rc -> {

                options.addHeader("method",
"obtainAllCustomers");


vertx.eventBus().send("com.zanclus.customer", null,
options, reply ->

handleReply(reply, rc));

            });
```

```
vertx.createHttpServer().requestHandler(router::acc
ept).listen(8080);

    } else {

        log.error("Deployment of worker verticles

has failed.",

res.cause());

        }

    });

}
```

Although the implemented routes are the same, the code for implementation of these is not the same. In our previous case, we had used calls to the blockingHandler. In this case, we have use of the async handlers which usually events on our event bus. The vertices have no database processing anymore.

The database processing has been moved to the worker vertical, and this has multiple instances for the purpose of handling multiple requests in a thread-safe and parallel manner. We have also registered a callback which will be triggered once the events have been replied to and the appropriate response will be sent to the client which has made the request.

The logic for handling database processing and error handling has been implemented as shown below:

@Override

public void start() throws Exception {

vertx.eventBus().consumer("com.zanclus.customer")
.handler(this::handleDatabaseRequest);
}

public void

handleDatabaseRequest(Message<Object> msg) {

　　String method = msg.headers().get("method");

```java
DeliveryOptions options = new DeliveryOptions();
try {
    String retrieveValue;
    switch (method) {
        case "obtainAllCustomers":
            retrieveValue =
mapper.writeValueAsString(dao.findAll());
            msg.reply(retVal, options);
            break;
        case "obtainCustomer":
            Long id =
Long.parseLong(msg.headers().get("id"));
            retrieveValue =
mapper.writeValueAsString(dao.findOne(id));
            msg.reply(retrieveValue);
            break;
        case "newCustomer":
            retrieveValue = mapper.writeValueAsString(
                dao.save(
```

```java
            mapper.readValue(

((JsonObject)msg.body()).encode(),
Customer.class)));

        msg.reply(retrieveValue);

        break;

    default:

        log.error("An invalid method '" + method +
"'");

        options.addHeader("error", "An invalid
method '" + method + "'");

        msg.fail(1, "An invalid method");

    }

} catch (IOException | NullPointerException ex) {

    log.error("Problem when parsing JSON data.",
ex);

    msg.fail(2, e.getLocalizedMessage());

}

}
```

The verticals for the worker *"CustomerWorker"* will register the consumer for the messages on an event bus. The string for representing the address on the bus is arbitrary, but it is recommended that the naming structure which is to be used should be "reverse-tld," which ensures that used addresses are unique. Once a new message has been sent to that address, it will have to be delivered to only one of the worker vehicles.

The database work will be done after calling of the ***"handleDatabaseRequest,"*** and the processes of error handling and JSON serialization will also be done.

Your app will then be ready. You are now aware of how to use Vert.x so as to improve the efficiency and concurrency of your app without having to rewrite your full app.

Chapter 7- The Actor Model

This model was created in the year 1973, and its popularity has grown in the field of concurrent programming. In this model, an application has to be broken into small parts known as "*models*" which are then executed. These actors are then used for encapsulation of state and behavior of a part of an application

The first part in which the actor is defined makes it sound like an actor, in object-oriented design. However, communication, which is a third party distinguishes standard objects and an actor.

Actors do not directly interact with each other, but they do communicate through messages. The behavior of an actor is defined by the way it handles messages which it receives. You have to note that the state of any actor is always isolated from the system, and this is why an actor does not have to worry about issues to do with synchronization, such as modifying the state, and thread locking.

An actor model becomes more interesting when it comes to combination of multiple actors so as to get a supervisory hierarchy. Once the actors have been organized into an hierarchy, you can have parent actors which will manage the child actors, and the computations will be delegated to the child actors. If you manage to control the hierarchy of your application, it will become easy for you to make your application scalable and fault-tolerant.

The important thing about this is that the actors are not created directly, but the actor system is tasked with the creation of these. The object which is returned in such a case is not the actor itself, but it is a reference to the actor, usually referred to as an *"ActorRef."* The referencing to the actor is done via this ActorRef, and the messages are sent to the same. Once a failure has occurred, it becomes possible for you to restart the actor transparently. The actor is also managed in a transparent manner. The actor also finds it possible for it to maintain a state which is mutable, and it doesn't have to worry about the concurrent access to that.

Defining an Actor

To define an actor, one can use either their IDE or the Typesafe activator. The following steps can be followed for definition of an actor in the activator:

1. Select the tab for *"Code."*

2. Navigate to the directory "src/main/java or src/main/scala."

3. Add a new file by creating the + sign.

4. In the source directory, create the files "JavaMain.java" and "JavaBot.java" or "ScalaMain.scala" and "ScalaBot.scala." Add the following code to those files:

// Java code for file JavaMain.java

import akka.actor.ActorRef;

import akka.actor.Props;

```java
import akka.actor.ActorSystem;

public class JavaMain {

    public static void main(String[] args) {

        // Creating the actor system for 'helloakka'

        final ActorSystem system =
ActorSystem.create("helloakka");

        // Creating the 'AkkaBot' actor

        final ActorRef akkaBot =
system.actorOf(Props.create(AkkaBot.class),
"akkaBot");

        System.out.println("The Actor System for
JavaMain was created");

    }

}

// Java code for the JavaBot.java

import akka.actor.UntypedActor;

public class JavaBot extends UntypedActor {

    boolean moving = false;

    public void onReceive(Object message) {

        unhandled(message);

    }

}
```

```scala
//Scala code for the ScalaMain.scala
import akka.actor.{Props, ActorSystem}
object ScalaMain extends App {
  // Creating the 'helloakka' actor system
  val system = ActorSystem("helloakka")
  // Creating the 'akkaBot' actor
  val akkaBot =
system.actorOf(Props[ScalaAkkaBot],
"akkaBot")
println("The Actor System for ScalaMain was
created")
}
//Scala code for the ScalaBot.scala
import akka.actor.Actor
class ScalaBot extends Actor {
  var moving: Boolean = false
  def receive = {
    case msg => unhandled(msg)  }
}
```

Our initial implementation can be tested by running the code in the activator. Follow the steps given below:

1. Click on the *"Run"* tab in the activator.

2. Change the main class to be the main class which you have defined.

3. In the output presented on the left hand side, the output from the application will be displayed.

Creating Actors

Now that the actor has been defined, we can create its instance. In Akka, this is not done directly by use of the factory, by use of the *"new"* keyword. We will not get an instance of our actor, but it will be an ActorRef which will point to the actor instance.

With such a level of indirection, much power and flexibility will be added to the system. Location transparency is provided, which means that it is possible for the ActorRef to represent an instance of the actor which is running and maintain the same semantics.

Once we use the actor system for creation of an actor, the actor is directly created at the top of your hierarchy. The local Actor Context of the actor can also be used for the purpose of creating actors as children of other actors. The Actor Context will have information regarding the Actor System which is relevant to each of the actors, such as the relationship between the parent and the child.

Defining Messages

There is no public API in an actor in terms of the methods which you are able to invoke. The messages themselves can be of any type. Messages should be sent with good semantics and names, and their meaning should be specific to a particular domain, even in cases where you only need to wrap the data type. Public static classes can be used for us to achieve this in Java, while in Scala, we can do this using classes or case objects.

We want to begin by defining our messages in Java. The messages defined should be immutable to avoid the risk of sharing a state which is immutable between two actors which are different, as this can lead to the violation of the Actor Model. This is shown in the code given below:

```java
public enum Direction { FORWARD, BACKWARDS,
RIGHT, LEFT }

public static class Motion {

    public final Direction direction;

    public Motion(Direction direction) { this.direction
= direction; }
}

public static class Stop {}

public static class ObtainRobotState {}

public static class RobotState {

    public final Direction direction;

    public final boolean moving;

    public RobotState(Direction direction, boolean
moving) {

        this.direction = direction;

        this.moving = moving;

    }

}
```

In Scala, case objects and case classes make excellent messages, because these are immutable and they have support for pattern matching, and we will take advantage of this when we are processing the messages which the actor has received. Consider the example given below:

```
object Scala {
sealed abstract class Direction
case object FORWARD extends Direction
case object BACKWARDS extends Direction
case object RIGHT extends Direction
case object LEFT extends Direction
case class Motion(direction:Direction)
case object Stop
case object ObtainRobotState
case class RobotState(direction: Direction, moving: Boolean)
}
```

It is also good for us to tell the actor to do something. Asynchronous message passing is used for the purpose of all communication with actors. The actor will do nothing, unless you command it to do something. For you to do this, you have to tell the actor to send a message. If the message is sent asynchronously, the sender of the message will not have to wait for the message to be processed by the recipient. This time can then be utilized for doing something else constructive.

We want to illustrate how this can be done. Let us begin by defining the *"onReceive"* method for the *"Motion"* and *"Stop"* messages. For those doing it in java, make the following changes to the file *"JavaBot.java."*

// Add the field given below:

Direction direction = Direction.FORWARD

// Changing the onReceive method to be as follows

```
public void onReceive(Object message) {

    if (message instanceof Motion) {

        direction = ((Motion) message).direction;

        moving = true;

    }

    else if (message instanceof Stop) {

        moving = false;

    }

    else {

        unhandled(message);

    }

}
```

In the case of Scala, the following changes should be made to the ScalaBott:

/// add the import given below inside ScalaBot class:

import ScalaBot._

// Add the field given below

```
var direction: Direction = FORWARD

//Change the method onReceive to be as follows:

def receive = {

  case Motion(newDirection) =>

    moving = true

    direction = newDirection

    println(s"I am currently moving $direction")

  case Stop =>

    moving = false

    println(s"I have stopped moving")

  case msg => unhandled(msg)

}
```

Testing of the apps can then be done. In the file *"JavaMain.java,"* add the following code:

```
akkaBot.tell(new
JavaBot.Move(JavaBot.Direction.FORWARD),
ActorRef.noSender());
```

```
akkaBot.tell(new
JavaBot.Move(JavaBot.Direction.BACKWARDS),
ActorRef.noSender());

akkaBot.tell(new JavaBot.Stop(),

ActorRef.noSender());
```

For Scala users, add the following piece of code to the file
ScalaMainscala:

```
akkaBot ! ScalaBot.Move(ScalaBot.FORWARD)

akkaBot ! ScalaBot.Move(ScalaBot.BACKWARDS)

akkaBot ! ScalaBot.Stop
```

Just run the application, and logging regarding the same app
will be observed.

Actor Hierarchies

Actor hierarchies define the real power of actors. An actor hierarchy is created once a parent actor has defined a child and takes over the role of supervising them. With such a structure, no failures will be cascaded.

The process of creation of child actors is the same as that of creation of top level actors, but the difference comes in the context in which the child is created. The context of an actor is the area in the actor hierarchy in which the actor lives. We want to demonstrate this by creating a Bot master which will then create several children.

Create the class JavaMaster, which will be used for creating several children in our constructor. The code for the class should be as shown below:

```
import akka.actor.UntypedActor;

import akka.actor.ActorRef;

import akka.actor.Props;

public class JavaMaster extends UntypedActor {

  public JavaMaster() {

    for (int index = 0; index < 10; index++) {

      context().actorOf(Props.create(JavaBot.class));

    }

  }

  public void onReceive(Object message) {}

}
```

In the case of Scala, just create the class *"ScalaMaster"* with the following piece of code:

```
import akka.actor.{Props, Actor}

class ScalaMaster extends Actor {

  import ScalaMaster._
```

```scala
import ScalaBot._

for (index <- 1 to 10) {

  context.actorOf(Props[ScalaBot])

}

def receive = {

  case _ =>

}

}
```

In Java and Scala, we will have to obtain the local actor context and then create new actors within that context. At this point, it is possible for the master to interact directly with the children.

Modify the onReceive method in java to get the following:

```java
public void onReceive(Object message) {

  if (message instanceof StartChildBots) {

    for (ActorRef child : getContext().getChildren()) {
```

```
        System.out.println("The    Master    has    started

moving " + child);

        child.tell(new
JavaBot.Move(JavaBot.Direction.FORWARD),
getContext().self());

    }

        System.out.println("The  Master  has  started  the
children bots");

    }

}

public static class StartChildBots {}
```

In Scala, the case object can be added as follows:

```
  object ScalaMaster {

  case object StartChildBots

}
```

Modify your receive function to get the following:

```
def receive = {

  case StartChildBots =>

    context.children.foreach { child =>

      println(s"child=$child")

      child ! Move(FORWARD)

    }

    println("The master has started the children bots.")

}
```

The above code will look for the context of the master bot for all of the children. The children will then be iterated upon, and a message sent to each child.

For this to be tested out, we have to modify our Akka bots so as to print out their path and make it easy for us to see the origin of the trace statements. The print statement in Java should be changed to the following:

System.out.println(self().path() + " is currently moving " + direction);

The path of the current actor, which is to be obtained with the above code, should be as follows:

akka://helloakka/user/akkaMaster/$f

$f represents the name of the actor. Since an explicit name was not given to this actor, Akka chose a random name and then assigned it to the name. From what we can see, our actor is just a child of the akkaMaster.

Fault Tolerance

With actor hierarchies, we can build systems which are self-healing and fault-tolerant. For this to be done, we have to isolate the errors from the child actors, and then monitor the actors for any failures which might occur. Failures are very normal in apps, and there are a number of reasons which can cause this.

In Reactive programming, failures can be dealt with in two ways. In the first method, we can customize the supervision strategy. Each actor is associated with a supervision strategy which usually defines the way it will handle failures and its children. In the case of an exception, the default supervisor strategy is to restart your actor. However, it is possible for us to override the strategy so as to specify a new behavior.

In the second mechanism on how to manage failures associated with children, the parent can choose to add watches to its children. Once the child has been terminated, the parent will have to receive a terminated message. Suppose we need to perform some special processing in case the child robot has been changed. For this to be done, we just have to add a watch once the robot has been created.

In Java, you just have to add the following code to the constructor:

```
ActorRef child =
context().actorOf(Props.create(JavaBot.class));

context().watch(child);
```

The case of receiving the terminated message can then be handled on the onReceive method. This is shown in the code given below:

```java
else if (message instanceof Terminated) {

    System.out.println("The child has stopped ... now starting a new one");

    ActorRef child =

context().actorOf(Props.create(JavaBot.class));

    context().watch(child);
}
```

The following code could have been used in Scala:

```scala
val child = context.actorOf(Props[ScalaBot])

context.watch(child)
```

The receive method can then be modified for the purpose of handling the terminated message. This can be done as follows:

```scala
case akka.actor.Terminated(ref) =>
```

```
println("The child has stopped ... now starting a new
one")

val child = context.actorOf(Props[ScalaBot])

context.watch(child)
```

Our aim is now to make the child fail randomly. To do this in Java, we just have to add a field to the Motion message handler in the class JavaBolt as shown below:

```
Random rand = new java.util.Random();

int nextInt = rand.nextInt(10);

if ( (nextInt % 2) == 0) {

    context().stop(self());

}
```

In the case of Acala, the following Motion message handler can be added to the class ScalaBott:

```scala
val random = scala.util.Random
println(s"${self.path} currently moving $direction")
if ((random.nextInt(10) % 10) == 0) {
  context.stop(self)
}
```

Chapter 8- Reactive Extensions

C++ provides us with RxCpp (Reactive Extensions for Native), which is a library which programmers can use for the purpose of composing event-based and asynchronous programs by use of observable sequences. This library can be added to the included files as shown below:

```
#include "rxcpp/rx.hpp"
using namespace rxcpp;
using namespace rxcpp::operators;
using namespace rxcpp::sources;
namespace rxcpp::util;

#include <regex>
#include <random>
using namespace std;

int main()
```

```cpp
{
    random_device rd;   //a non-deterministic
generator

    mt19937 gen(rd());

    uniform_int_distribution<> dist(4, 18);


    // for the purpose of testing, produce a byte stream
which form the lines of text
    auto bytes = range(1, 10) |
        flat_map([&](int i){
            auto body = from((uint8_t)('A' + i)) |
                repeat(dist(gen)) |
                as_dynamic();
            auto delim = from((uint8_t)'\r');
            return from(body, delim) | concat();
        }) |
        window(17) |
        flat_map([](observable<uint8_t> w){
            return w |
                reduce(
                    vector<uint8_t>(),
```

```cpp
        [](vector<uint8_t>& v, uint8_t b){

            v.push_back(b);

            return move(v);

        }) |

    as_dynamic();

}) |

tap([](vector<uint8_t>& v){

    // print input packet of bytes

    copy(v.begin(), v.end(),

ostream_iterator<long>(cout, " "));

    cout << endl;

});

    // recovering the lines of the text from our byte
stream

    // creating the strings split on \r

  auto strings = bytes |

    concat_map([](vector<uint8_t> v){

        string s(v.begin(), v.end());

        regex delim(R"/(\r)/");

        sregex_token_iterator cursor(s.begin(),
s.end(), delim, {-1, 0});
```

```cpp
      sregex_token_iterator end;

      vector<string> splits(cursor, end);

      return iterate(move(splits));

    }) |
    filter([](string& s){

      return !s.empty();

    });


  // grouping the strings by line
  int group = 0;
  auto linewindows = strings |
    group_by(

      [=](string& s) mutable {

        return s.back() == '\r' ? group++ : group;

      });


  // reducing the strings for the line into one string
  auto lines = linewindows |
    flat_map([](grouped_observable<int, string> w){
```

```
    return w | sum();
});


// printing the result
lines |
    subscribe<string>(println(cout));
return 0;
}
```

JavaScript also provides us with the RxJS (Reactive Extensions for JavaScript), which is a library programmers can use for the purpose of composing event-based and asynchronous programs by use for fluent query operators and observable sequences in JavaScript. Consider the JavaScript code given below:

```
/* Getting the stock data somehow */

const source = getAsyncStockData();


const subscription = source

  .filter(quote => quote.price > 50)

  .map(quote => quote.price)

  .forEach(price => console.log(`Prices which are
higher than $50: ${price}`);
```

Suppose the data was to come like an event such as a stream, the query could have been written so that it can iterate over the data, and very little change will be needed as shown below:

```
/* Getting the stock data somehow */

const source = getAsyncStockData();

const subscription = source

  .filter(quote => quote.price > 50)

  .map(quote => quote.price)

  .subscribe(
```

```
    price => console.log(`The prices higher than $50:
${price}`),

    err => console.log(`Something wrong happened:
${err.message}`);

  );

subscription.dispose();
```

The difference is that the errors have been handled inside our subscription. Since we don't need to receive the data as it streams in, we have just called the *"dispose"* on our subscription. You have to note that we have called the *"dispose"* rather than *"forEach."* Although any of these can be used, we recommend that you use*"subscribe."*

Why RxJS?

Promises are a very good way for us to solve asynchronous problems such as querying for services with XMLHttpRequest, and in this case, we expect we value before completion.

We need to demonstrate this by creating an auto-completion system for the user. Let us begin by referencing the necessary JavaScript files:

```
<script src="https://code.jquery.com/jquery.js"></script>
<script src="rx.lite.js"></script>
```

We now need to get the user input from our user, listen to keyup event by use of the method "Rx.Observable.fromEvent". Consider the code given below:

```
const $input = $('#input');

const $results = $('#results');


/* get the value only from each of the key up */

var keyups = Rx.Observable.fromEvent($input,
'keyup')

  .pluck('target', 'value')

  .filter(text => text.length > 2 );


/* The input should be debounced for 500ms */

var debounced = keyups

  .debounce(500 /* ms */);


/* getting only the distinct values now, so the arrows
and other control characters should be eliminated */

var distinct = debounced

  .distinctUntilChanged();
```

It is possible for us to bind directly to Promise A+ in RxJS, through the method "Rx.Observable.fromPromise." We can also choose to return it directly and the RxJS will directly wrap it for us as shown below:

```
function searchWikipedia (name) {
  return $.ajax({
    url: 'https://en.wikipedia.org/w/api.php',
    dataType: 'jsonp',
    data: {
      action: 'opensearch',
      format: 'json',
      search: term
    }
  }).promise();
}
```

In the above code, we are just searching from the Wikipedia. After creation of the above, the input can be tied together and the service queried. In such a case, we have to use the method "flatMapLatest" for getting the value, and we will not introduce any order sequence calls. This is shown below:

```
var suggestions = distinct
  .flatMapLatest(searchWikipedia);
```

We can then call the *"subscribe"* on the observable sequence, and then start to pull our data. Consider the code given below:

```
suggestions.subscribe(
  data => {
   $results
    .empty()
    .append($.map(data[1], value =>
$('<li>').text(value)))
```

```
},
error=> {
 $results
  .empty()
  .append($('<li>'))
   .text('Error:' + error);
});
```

Chapter 10- A Sample App

We want to use JavaScript and RxJS to create a sample app.

In Twitter, you always find the *"follow"* button which suggests for you the accounts which you can follow.

We want to create an app which will imitate the core features of this button. On startup, this should load the data for the accounts from the API and then display the necessary suggestions. Once you click on *"Refresh,"* three other account suggestions should be loaded.

Request and Response

We want to load three accounts on startup. To implement this, we have to send a request, receive a response and then render the response. Let us begin by subscribing to the stream that we have:

requestStream.subscribe(function(requestUrl) {

  // executing the request

  jQuery.getJSON(requestUrl,

function(responseData) {

    // ...

  });

}

We have used the JQuery Ajax Callback so as to handle the asynchronicity of our request operation. However, we can use Rx to handle our asynchronous streams of data. Consider the code given below:

```
requestStream.subscribe(function(requestUrl) {

  // executing the request

  var responseStream =
Rx.Observable.create(function (observer) {

    jQuery.getJSON(requestUrl)

    .done(function(response) {

observer.onNext(response); })

    .fail(function(jqXHR, status, error) {

observer.onError(error); })

    .always(function() { observer.onCompleted(); });

});


responseStream.subscribe(function(response) {

  // use the response to do something

});
```

}

The function *"map(f)"* will take an input stream, perform *f* on it and then produces another value. This is demonstrated in the code given below:

var responseMetastream = requestStream

  .map(function(requestUrl) {

    return Rx.Observable.fromPromise(jQuery.getJSON(requestUrl));

  });

The *"metastream"*_ just represents a stream of streams. In this case, each emitted value will still become a stream. This can be thought to work in the same way as pointers. Consider the code given below:

```
var responseStream = requestStream

.flatMap(function(requestUrl) {

  return
Rx.Observable.fromPromise(jQuery.getJSON(reques
tUrl));

});
```

You should note that a metastream response may be confusing, and it may end up not helping you. In our case, we just need a simple stream made up of responses, and each of the emitted value should be a JSON object, as opposed to being a "promise" of a JSON object.

Since we now have a response stream, the data which is received can be rendered as shown below:

```
responseStream.subscribe(function(response) {
  // render the `response` to the our DOM the way you
wish

});
```

At this point, your whole code should be as follows:

```
var requestStream =
Rx.Observable.just('https://api.SourceName.com/us
ers');

var responseStream = requestStream

 .flatMap(function(requestUrl) {

  return
Rx.Observable.fromPromise(jQuery.getJSON(reques
tUrl));

 });


responseStream.subscribe(function(response) {

 // render the `response` to your DOM the way you
wish

});
```

Refresh Button

After clicking on this button, the request stream is expected to emit a new URL, and we will get a new response. We expect to have a stream of the click events on our refresh button, and the request stream also needs to be changed so that it can depend on a refresh click stream. RxJS provides us with tools for making the Observables from the event listeners. This is shown in the code given below:

```
var refreshButton =
document.querySelector('.refresh');

var refreshClickStream =
Rx.Observable.fromEvent(refreshButton, 'click');
```

Since our refresh click event will not carry with it any API URL, each click should be mapped to an actual URL. The request stream can now be changed to our refresh click stream which has been mapped to our API endpoint by use of a random offset parameter each time we do this. Consider the code given below:

```
var requestStream = refreshClickStream
  .map(function() {
    var randomOffset =
Math.floor(Math.random()*400);
    return 'https://api.SiteName.com/users?since=' +
randomOffset;
  });
```

Requests do not happen after starting the app, but these only happen once we have clicked on the refresh button. But in our case, we need this to happen in both cases, after a click on the refresh button and after a webpage has been loaded.

You are aware of how a separate stream can be made for these two behaviors. The code given below demonstrates this:

```
var requestOnRefreshStream = refreshClickStream
  .map(function() {
    var randomOffset =
Math.floor(Math.random()*400);
    return 'https://api.SiteName.com/users?since=' +
randomOffset;
  });
```

```
var startupRequestStream =
Rx.Observable.just('https://api.SiteName.com/users'
);
```

The work then becomes easy for us:

```
var requestOnRefreshStream = refreshClickStream
  .map(function() {
```

```
   var randomOffset =
Math.floor(Math.random()*400);

   return 'https://api.SiteName.com/users?since=' +
randomOffset;

 });


var startupRequestStream =
Rx.Observable.just('https://api.SiteName.com/users'
);

var requestStream = Rx.Observable.merge(

 requestOnRefreshStream, startupRequestStream

);
```

If you do not need to use the immediate streams, this can be

implemented as follows:

```
var requestStream = refreshClickStream

 .map(function() {

  var randomOffset =

Math.floor(Math.random()*500);
```

```
   return 'https://api.SiteName.com/users?since=' +
randomOffset;
 })
```

```
.merge(Rx.Observable.just('https://api.SiteName.co
m/users'));
```

To make it shorter and more readable, implement it as follows:

```
var requestStream = refreshClickStream

 .map(function() {

  var randomOffset =

Math.floor(Math.random()*500);

   return 'https://api.SiteName.com/users?since=' +
randomOffset;

 })

 .startWith('https://api.SiteName.com/users');
```

However, according to the code we have, the output stream we get will have an "x" at the beginning. To solve this, the code can be altered as follows:

```
var requestStream =

refreshClickStream.startWith('click me')

 .map(function() {

  var randomOffset =

Math.floor(Math.random()*400);

  return 'https://api.SiteName.com/users?since=' +
randomOffset;

 });
```

We can then use streams so as to model our three suggestions. At this point, once you have clicked on the refresh button, the three suggestions won't be cleared. New suggestions will only come once a response has been received, but the interface will not be good with this. Solve this using the following code:

```
refreshClickStream.subscribe(function() {

 // clearing the 3 suggestion for DOM elements

});
```

The suggestion can be modeled as a stream using the following code:

```
var sug1Stream = responseStream

  .map(function(listUsers) {

    // getting one random user from our list

    return listUsers[Math.floor(Math.random()*listUsers.length)];

  });
```

This can also be implemented as follows so as to map it to null:

```
var sug1Stream = responseStream

  .map(function(listUsers) {

    // getting one random user from our list

    return

    listUsers[Math.floor(Math.random()*listUsers.length)];

});
```

```
})
.merge(
  refreshClickStream.map(function(){ return null; })
);
```

This should be interpreted as no data, and the UI element will be hidden:

```
sug1Stream.subscribe(function(suggestion) {
  if (suggestion === null) {
    // hiding the first suggestion of DOM element
  }
  else {
    // showing the first suggestion of DOM element
    // and the render the data
  }
});
```

Closing the Suggestions

Each suggestion box has to have an "x" symbol which when clicked, the suggestion will be closed.

```
var c1Button = document.querySelector('.close1');

var c1ClickStream =
Rx.Observable.fromEvent(close1Button, 'click me');

var requestStream =

refreshClickStream.startWith('click')

  .merge(c1ClickStream)

  .map(function() {

   var randomOffset =
Math.floor(Math.random()*400);

   return 'https://api.SiteName.com/users?since=' +

randomOffset;

  });
```

We now need to get a response once we have clicked on the close button. This can be implemented as follows:

```
var sug1Stream = c1ClickStream
  .combineLatest(responseStream,
    function(click, listUsers) {
      return
listUsers[Math.floor(Math.random()*listUsers.length
)];
    }
  )
  .merge(
    refreshClickStream.map(function(){ return null; })
  )
  .startWith(null);
```

You will then be done. The complete code for the app should be as follows:

```
var refreshButton =

document.querySelector('.refresh');

var refreshClickStream =
Rx.Observable.fromEvent(refreshButton, 'click');


var cButton1 = document.querySelector('.close1');

var c1ClickStream =

Rx.Observable.fromEvent(cButton1, 'click');


var requestStream =

refreshClickStream.startWith('click me')

  .map(function() {

    var randomOffset =

Math.floor(Math.random()*400);

    return 'https://api.MySite.com/users?since=' +

randomOffset;

  });


var responseStream = requestStream

  .flatMap(function (requestUrl) {
```

```javascript
    return Rx.Observable.fromPromise($.ajax({url:
requestUrl}));
  });


var sug1Stream = close1ClickStream.startWith('click
me')
  .combineLatest(responseStream,
    function(click, listUsers) {
      return
listUsers[Math.floor(Math.random()*listUsers.length
)];
    }
  )
  .merge(
    refreshClickStream.map(function(){ return null; })
  )
  .startWith(null);


sug1Stream.subscribe(function(suggestion) {
  if (suggestion === null) {
```

```
	}
	else {
	}
});
```

Conclusion

We have come to the end of this guide. You must have grasped the important aspects of Reactive programming. This type of programming is very important when it comes to propagation of changes and data flows in an app. You should also have learned how to handle the callback hell. Futures and promises are very important in Reactive programming. Futures greatly help you in the representation of the output that you get from an asynchronous operation. These have been discussed in this guide. Explicit and implicit declarations are very important, and each should be applied in the correct context. Vert.x is a tool which you can use for the purpose of doing Reactive programming, so learn how to use it. Actors are always organized into a hierarchy. It will be good for you to know that parents and children work in an actor hierarchy.

www.ingramcontent.com/pod-product-compliance
Lightning Source LLC
Chambersburg PA
CBHW060943050326
40689CB00012B/2556